The Conspiracy That You Miss Me

poems about love, grief, and ancient aliens

Audrey Jacobs

BookLeaf
Publishing

India | USA | UK

Dedication

To J

for always listening to my bad notes app poetry

Preface

In this book you'll find raspberries that taste like regret, skies that refuse to meet your gaze, and the usual ramblings of someone who has lost something and hasn't learned how to accept it yet.

I hope it resonates with you.

Acknowledgements

I'd like to thank the Codex Gigas, Yellowstone National Park, The Watcher, The Backseat Lovers, The 1975, and Ancient Aliens for shaping my poetry and my view of the world.

Raspberry Seeds

I chew desire and it sticks in my teeth like raspberry
seeds.

I try not to tell you, I try to tell you.
I hope you read my face
in this light. I bite my cheek until it's bleeding
or until you're gone for the night.

it tastes like rasberries
when I spit into the sink.

it's still under my tongue in the morning.

Anthropology

Turn, and Orion's cold hand is on his bow,
or don't turn, and the stars turn anyway,
revolving around you.

Create an ancient culture with me, we'll believe
in what we see and then make up the rest,
something interesting, something to
draw on the cave wall.

I don't know how to grieve you. I don't want to
make up the ceremony by myself.

Turn, and I'm right behind you, walking the trail
to Dana Point, it's summer and the sky is full of
triangles.
Every three points make a triangle,
is what you used to say,
and they can't all be summer.
But they're warm, and winking at me.

Or don't turn, and I'll place the stones in a circle
or a line, or whatever I can still see in the dark.
Every circle makes a bigger ring, around
you, the whole of the thing,

and the sky isn't full with grief, it just keeps getting bigger
to fill more in,
the universe expanding above us.

Turn, and Orion's hand is on his bow
as above, so below,
and the rest is the same old story.

Grocery Shopping Before the Execution

If you need me I'm standing in front of the grapes
trying to remember how you smell but I'm
forgetting you.

I have a recurring dream where you pass me
in the bread aisle
brush against my arm
to send a current down my spine

and yes, it's like being executed,
one last moment of feeling alive.

Lucid Dreaming

I go to sleep exactly on time,
don't want to be early to dinner, but you
show up late and with a bad taste in your mouth
you keep saying my name when it's not scripted.

so I throw the spoon down and say
I hated that brown quilt and how it never
kept me warm so you had to
do the job yourself,

and I can do the job myself,
waking up and putting the orange juice back in the
fridge, waking up and not wondering what blanket
you're under now, and who is keeping your hands
warm and your toes frozen over.

I'm going off script but I need to find a way to phrase
"I forgive you and I still don't forgive you,
and what is the view outside your bedroom window
when does the sun come inside,
and I'm sorry that your brother died"
before we both wake up.

The Grand Prismatic

you and I on the edge of the green summer river
the green canyon, the green river killer, the sky over
Yellowstone before the storm.

you can be the grand prismatic spring
I'm circling, trying to memorize the colors
in your eyes, my reflection in the pool,
bright blue, pretty
alive, and the rain pours in the sunroof as
you watch my hair soak through,
like you're drowning and I'm still
distracting you.

Lunch For My Ghost

Turkey on sourdough,
orange juice on the side.
I think that was just the way
you liked it.

Lately you're my ghost,
get comfortable,
drop your sweater on the floor.

But leave me alone in my dreams,
just standing in the back of the room
like you have nothing to say to me.

Lately I hear you like the song my
roommate is playing in the other
room, the ghost in you,
by the Counting Crows,
an 80's outro just taking forever
to fade out.

Come on man,
shut that off.

Good Grief

I was never very good to you.
You lose something, you get up off your knees
so you can scream at God a little louder.

He's so serene it's almost like silence.
God should yell.
God should admit to his mistakes.

I just lie there in the silence
crying and crying into my ears.

Alexander the Great

You step on yourself and you give way,
a clay sculpture of Alexander the Great but
no one is left who remembers what you looked like
when you were alive.

I'm still here, even if I'm no longer alive,
A ghost you know or a ghost you don't,
And is that really my face from the side?

Haunting Me In The Bread Aisle Again

Are all our songs repurposed in your mind
as grocery store background noise
that you don't recognize?
A green canyon that you don't recognize.

I won't say it's the way
I imagined it, but it is the way that it is.

I see you in the light blue parts of the sky
that are the most far away in my painting.
I'm painting again.
I'm flying a kite.

It was warm but November hit
me like it always does and
I hope you still remember it the way it was.

10. The Watcher

are you watching?

in my dream you're always two blue eyes on me,
hands by your sides,
and I could make you leave but
I'm holding on to something
you said to me at the grand prismatic spring,

and is it something you can see in me?

studying the reflection in the orange thermal pool,
see if there's something here to lose
or just prehistoric evidence

three silent years and the trees still
stand protecting you
because when I look up,
the whole blue sky is
just reflecting you.

Kilby Girl

If you've forgotten me
can you pin your location?
can you take me there, I'll be in the backseat of your car
lover, just pretend I'm not even here.

I'll be the shape of the steam in the shower
while you run your hands through her hair,
come on, don't let me distract you.

Driving the road to Yellowstone,
geysers exploding in your left ear,
I'm exploding in your left ear,
but I know! I should know better.

And who knows you better these days than me?
Nobody, lover,
nobody.

Matcha Latte And A Walk Around The Lake

I think I've been living in someone else's dream
and in her body.

I keep grinding the sand between my fingertips
but I just can't feel it.
the color yellow is so aggressive and
why can't I learn to like something,
frisbee golf, a matcha latte, walking in a big circle.

I throw a rock in the lake.
Now what?
The root of the problem is
in the mud, dead as the rest of it.

Watercolor

The lights on the water
(water this down)
your hand next to mine
and I'm holding it down, that
rush of the space in between.

Red and blue in a teenagers dream
and I'm not throwing it up
before I finish the painting or at least until you've
left for art school.

And what are you dreaming of
these days?
Now that there's nothing left of me,
the rush of the fall from the plane, or
the force of a fist in your teeth?

New Year's Night

The spine of the street lamp is black as a dime
It leans back into darkness
And I into mine.

Ice Cap

Don't make me sleep,
don't make me roll over inside my own body all night.

You just stare at me.
I want a Van Gogh painting, I want to wake up as a
squid.

Okay, I think I regret it like
an injection of ice water in my serum,

like a film in the back of my throat.
I'll be up all night trying to swallow it down,
but we all know how that goes.

The Twin Problem

My finger on the mirror,
trying to get a look at the line between
my fears and my dreams,
two identical twins I'm trying to tell apart.

Yes! This one definitely has a freckle here,
or wait, was it the other one.

Codex Gigas

I hope when you paint it I'm the villian
not the victim, would hate if you had pity on me.

Give me red claws and two tongues to lick them
and I'll smile and say it looks like me.

This Must Be My Dream

One red leaf to stain the whole tree
Sun through the veins, like I can see
through my hand to the lightbulb.

If the tree is dead, but the leaves are alive,
then who is eating the sun?
Not me, so I throw a wine glass at you in my
dream, and I watch the way you're watching me
like I could see through the leaf.

But that's delusional.

Your hug goodbye, so aggressive, like you were
getting the momentum to push off of me.

You're dancing and I'm in my seat,
yes, it's that same stupid scene,
we've all seen how this goes!
Julia Roberts laughs and the credits play.

Still I'm watching you and you're watching me
and I'm turning my phone so you can't
see me look up the lyrics
to the song you're playing in the car.

Cutting The Worm In Two

A body takes a walk in the rain,
maybe it's me,
and can you punish yourself enough or is that like
unlimited territory?

My hands are empty and I left your apartment
too rushed,
running actually.

If God is a child,
then I am the worm on the sidewalk
that he will not touch.

It's muddy,
And I wore my uggs,
just to ruin something.

Year of the Rabbit

In my memory my dad is still a young man,
everything is still okay.
I'm trying to read my zodiac sign off
a napkin in the restaurant.
Outside the air is thick with snow, rabbit fur
he's driving us home to a brown house
we haven't sold yet.

Don't tell me yet, what happens next,
the snow is blanketing the night with a
silence that could be peace,
and I could be anything,
the ice on the road, the lampost,
the rabbit leaving tracks in the snow.

Inception

Maybe I don't have to miss you
and it's just something I make myself do.

Maybe no one is thinking of you but me tonight,
say it's only me tonight,
haunting you, hiding behind your sweaters in the closet.

And one last time in my dream,
no it's not the right thing but it's blue
your striped sweater,
so soft against my cheek,
so softly you say that *you'll leave*
me to my dreams.
Because that's all I wanted from you.

you know, of course,
that it's one dream to another,
and I'll miss you when you do

finally call off the haunt.